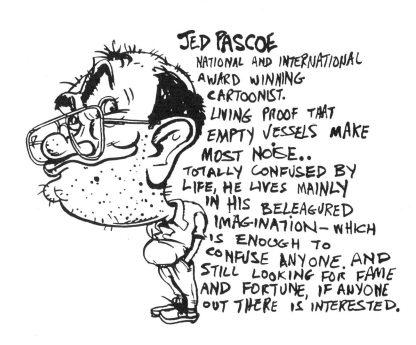

JED PASCOE
NATIONAL AND INTERNATIONAL
AWARD WINNING
CARTOONIST.
LIVING PROOF THAT
EMPTY VESSELS MAKE
MOST NOISE..
TOTALLY CONFUSED BY
LIFE, HE LIVES MAINLY
IN HIS BELEAGURED
IMAGINATION—WHICH
IS ENOUGH TO
CONFUSE ANYONE. AND
STILL LOOKING FOR FAME
AND FORTUNE, IF ANYONE
OUT THERE IS INTERESTED.

MEANWHILE BACK AT THE LEDGE
SO I SAID: "TAKE ME, FOR EXAMPLE... I'M OVER FORTY..." THEN SHE JUMPED!

THE PERFECT GIFT...

BIRTHDAYS ARE HELL WHEN YOU'RE ON A DIET...

OTHER WIVES SHRINK JUMPERS

I'LL SWEAR THESE YOUNG SALON ASSISTANTS ARE DEAF AS WELL AS BLIND...
... DOES THIS LOOK LIKE A PERM TO YOU ?

IT'S THE 'ONE OR TWO MATES' YOU INVITED ROUND ...

THAT'S THE LAST TIME I LET YOU TALK ME INTO GOING TEN-PIN BOWLING...

MY BIRTHDAY..

MY WHOLE
LIFE
FLASHED
BEFORE
MY EYES...

 AND I THOUGHT...

IS THAT ALL
THERE WAS
TO IT?